CAMILLE SAINT-SAËNS

PIANO CONCERTO No. 4
IN C MINOR, OP. 44

Music Minus One Piano

6044

Camille Saint-Saëns
Piano Concerto No. 4 in C minor

Piano Concerto No. 4 in C minor *(concerto pour piano en ut mineur),* Op. 44 by Camille Saint-Saëns, is the composer's most structurally innovative piano concerto. In one sense it is like a four-movement symphony, but these are grouped in pairs. That is, the piece is divided into two parts, each of which combines two main movements (Part 1: I. Moderate-tempo Theme and Variations in C Minor; II. Slower Theme and Variations in A-flat Major; Part 2: III. Scherzo in C Minor; IV. Finale in C Major). However, in each part there is a bridge-like transitional section, between the two main "movements" – for example, a fugal Andante in part II functions as an interlude between the two main sections.

The concerto begins with a gently mischievous chromatic subject, heard in dialogue between the strings and piano soloist, and continues in a creative thematic development similar to Saint-Saëns' Third Symphony. The composer demonstrates brilliant skill in employing the piano and orchestra almost equally. In the Andante, he moves to A-flat major with a chorale-like theme in the woodwinds (also strikingly similar to the tune of the Third Symphony's final section), and uses this as a platform on which to build a series of variations before bringing the movement to a quiet close.

The Allegro vivace begins again in C minor as a high-spirited scherzo, using material foreshadowed in the first movement. 2/4 and 6/8 are playfully juxtaposed throughout. At one point, the piano boldly leads the orchestra in an energetic 6/8 theme in E-flat major. Eventually the orchestra moves to a lush Andante, recapitulating the Andante section from the first movement. Rather suddenly, the piano climbs up to a flurry of double octave trills, and a climactic trumpet fanfare, leads to the jubilant finale based on a hymn-like theme in triple time. The concerto concludes with the piano, in glittering cascades, guiding the orchestra to a *fortissimo* close.

The piano concerto was premièred in 1875 with the composer as the soloist. The concerto is dedicated to Antoine Door, a professor of piano at the Vienna Conservatory. It continues to be one of Saint-Saëns' most popular piano concertos, second only to the Piano Concerto No. 2 in G minor. This highly inventive work, along with many others, does much to refute the caricature of a purely reactionary Saint-Saëns.

Music Minus One Piano

CAMILLE SAINT-SAËNS

PIANO CONCERTO NO. 4 IN C MINOR, OP. 44

CONTENTS

CAMILLE SAINT-SAËNS
PIANO CONCERTO No. 4 IN C MINOR, Op. 44

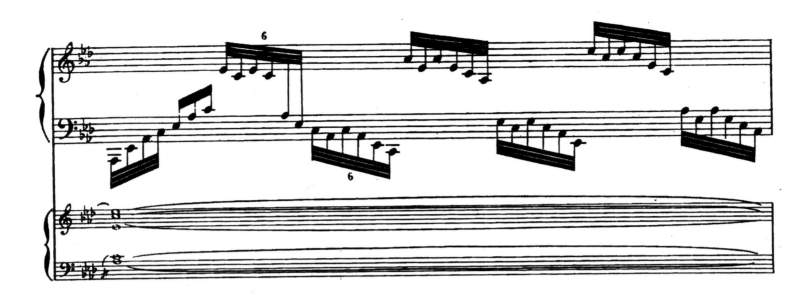

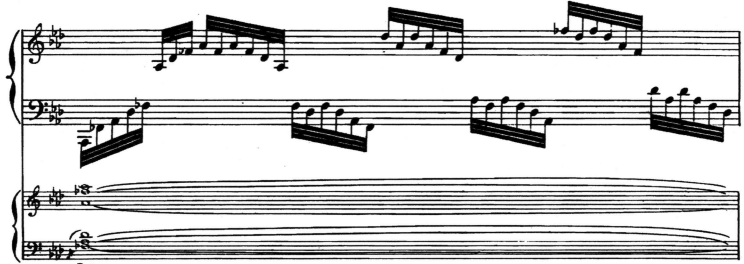

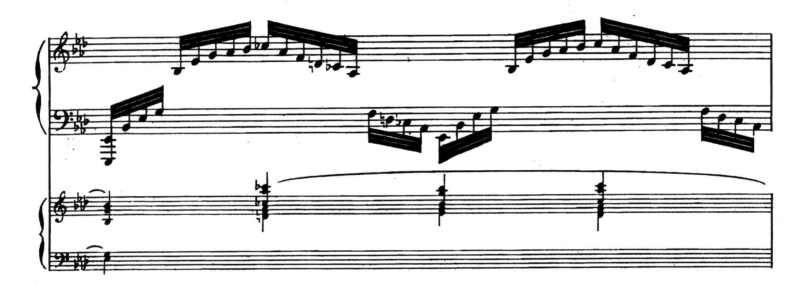

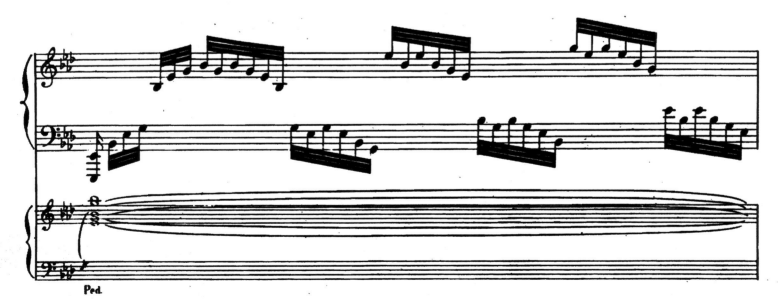

Ped.

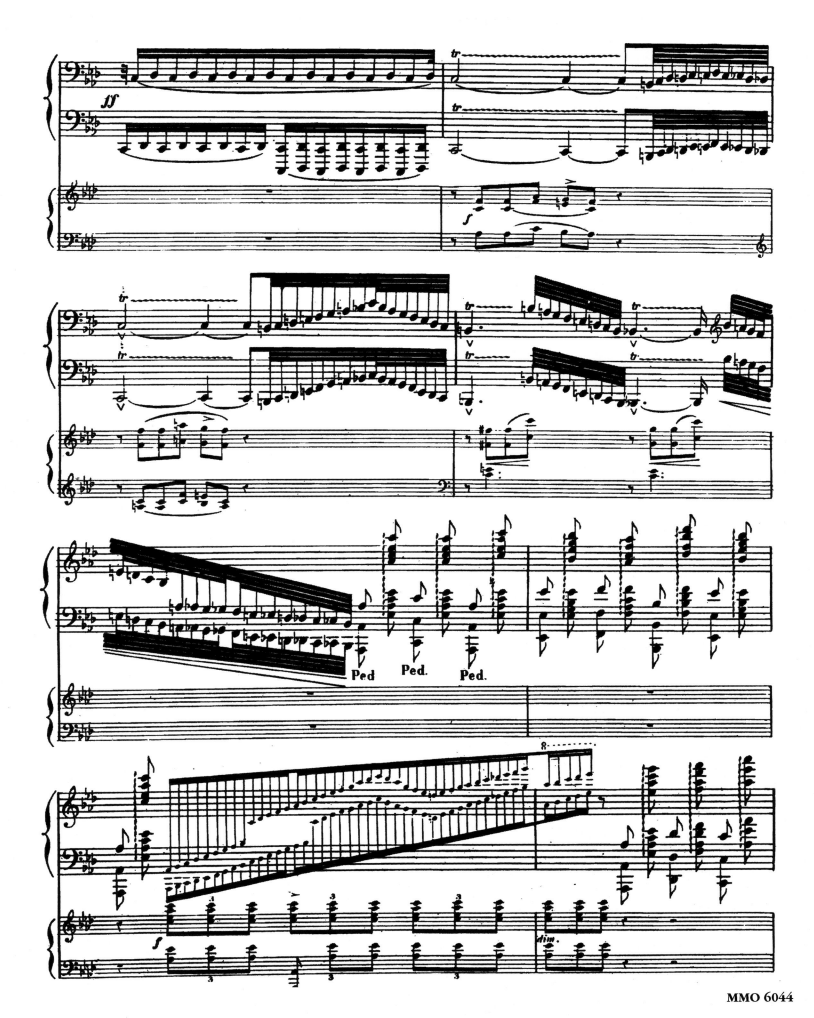

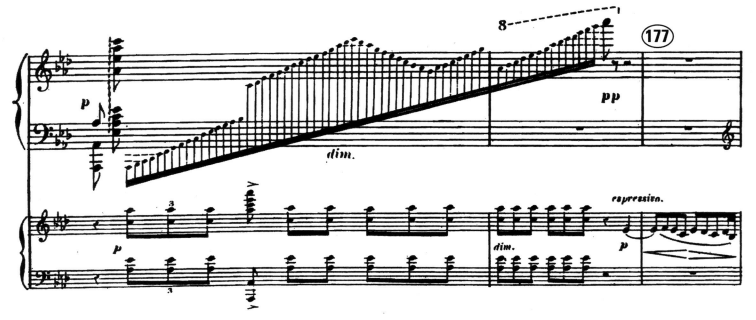

dolce tranquillo legato.

express.

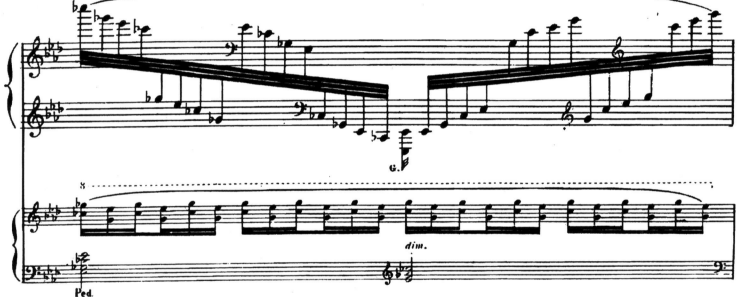

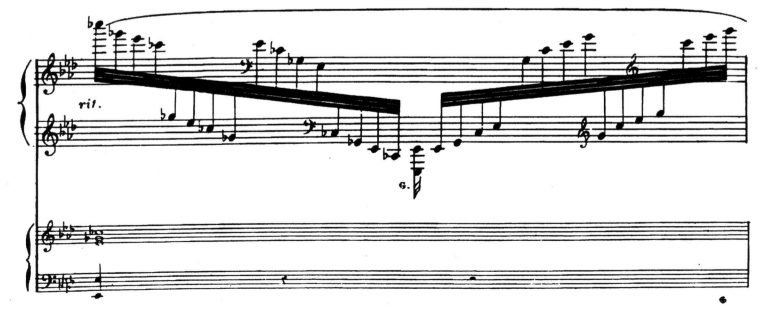

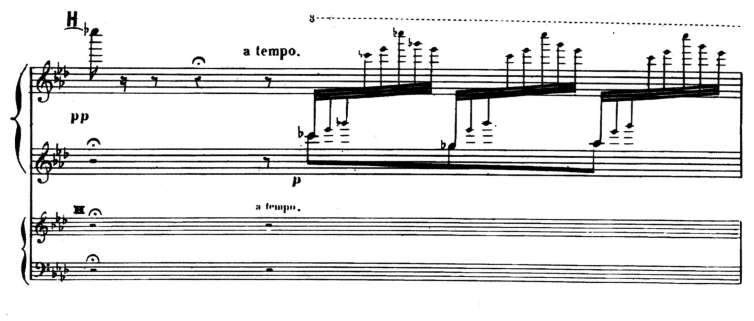

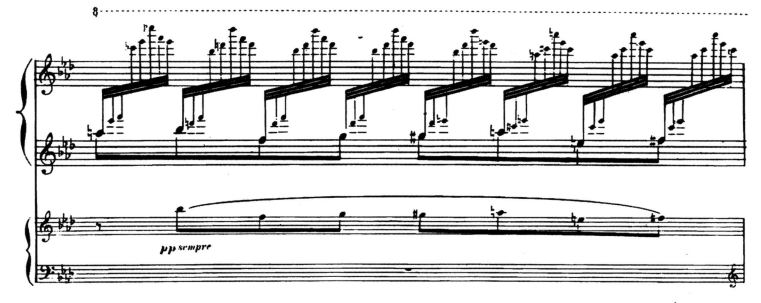

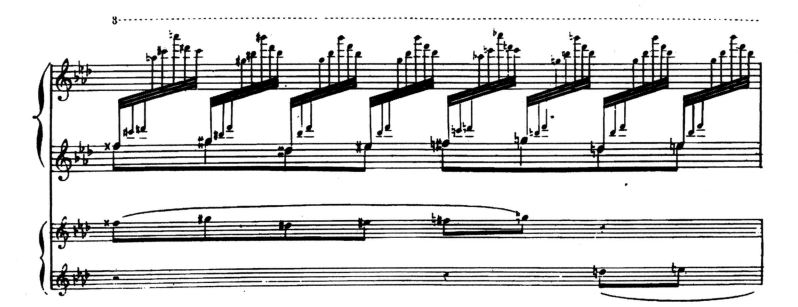

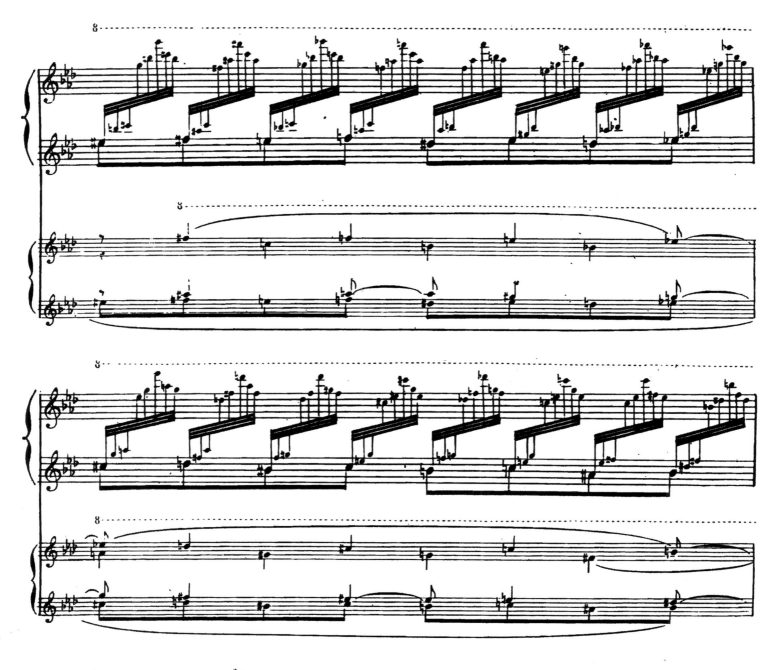

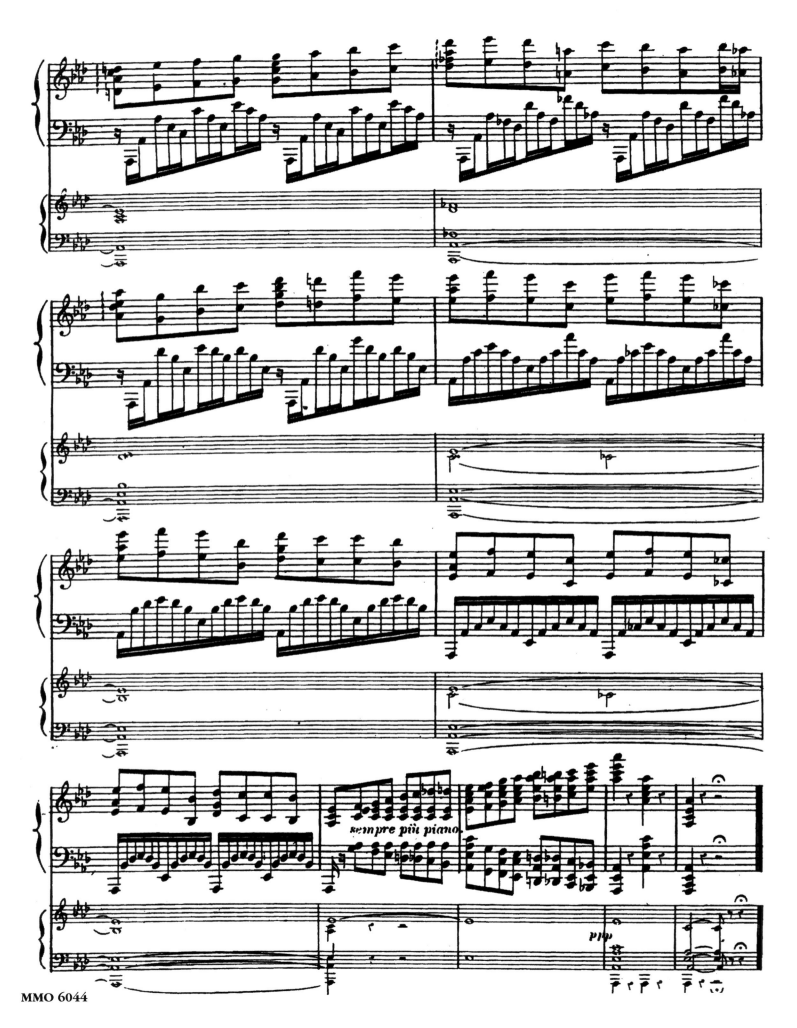

II

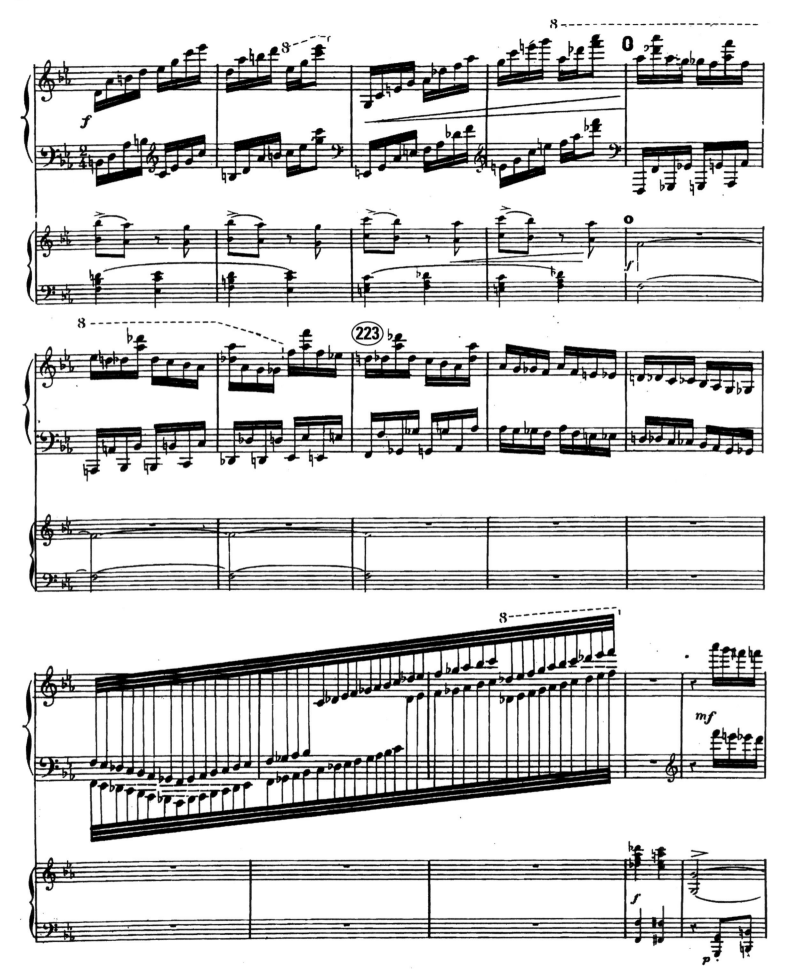

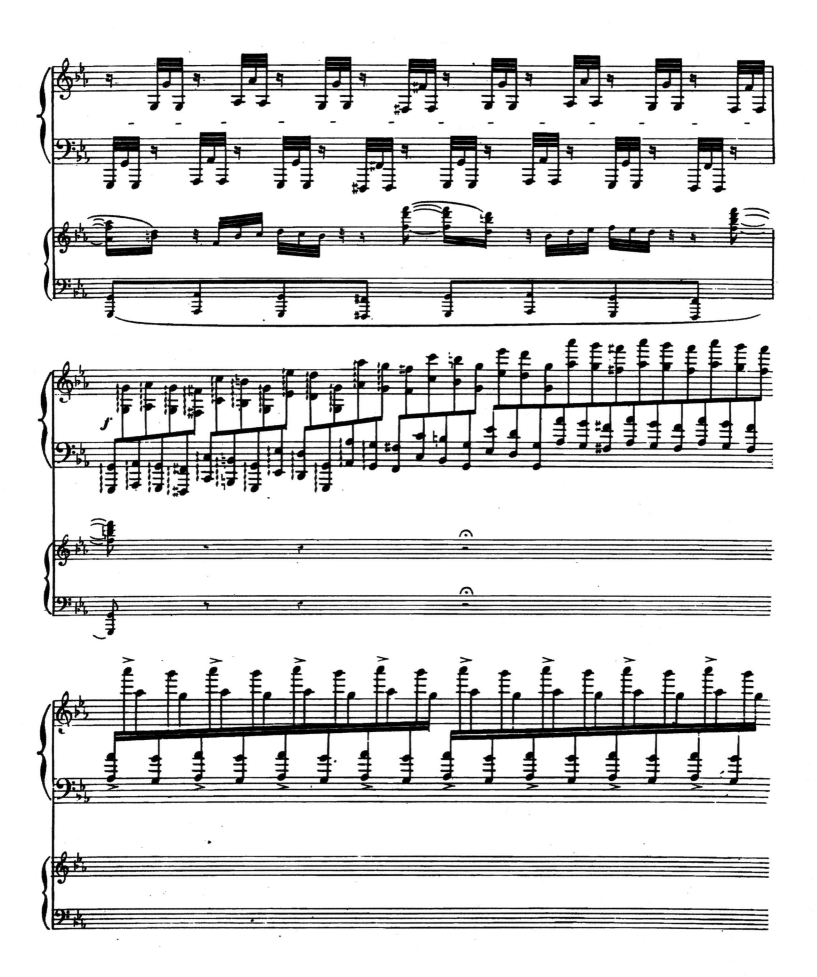

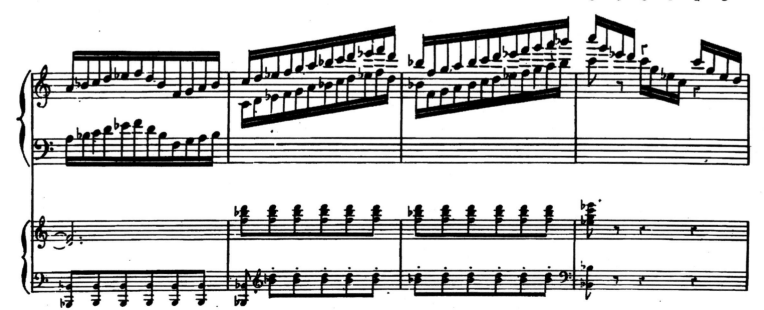

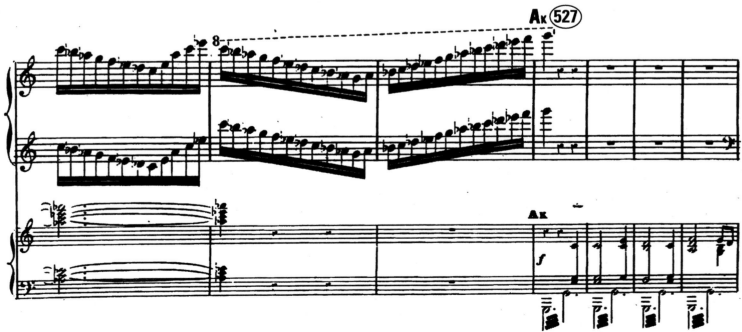

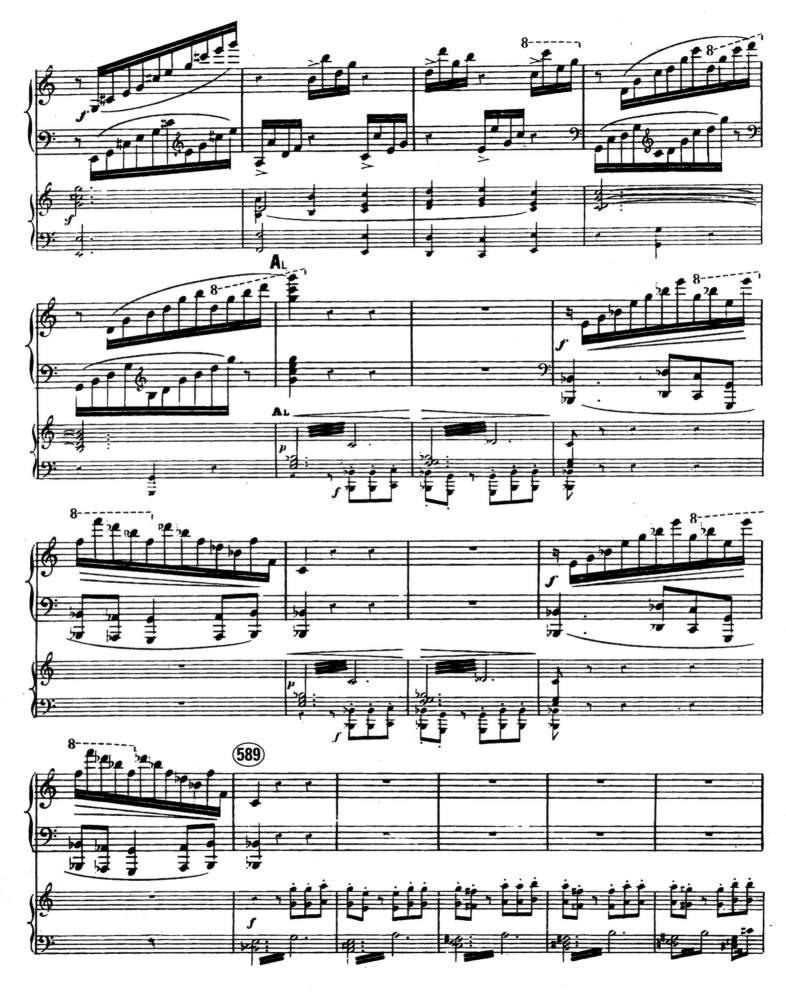

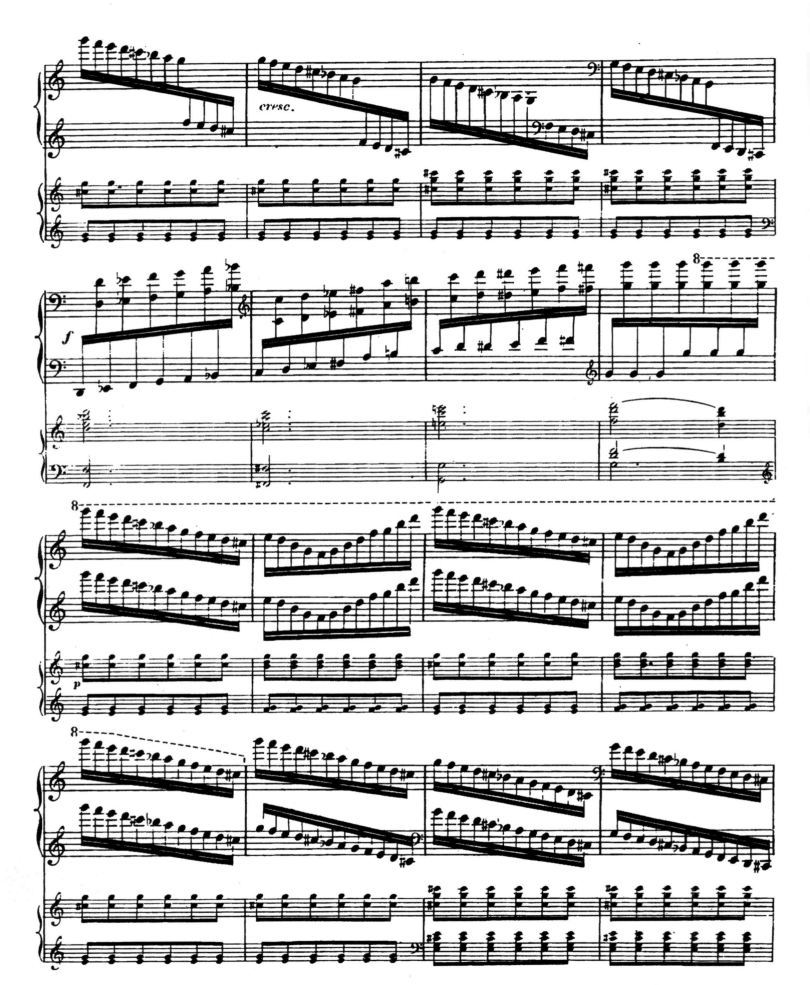

A WORLD OF PIANO MUSIC FROM MUSIC MINUS ONE
Quality Accompaniment Editions since 1950
www.musicminusone.com

Chamber Classics

____ ARENSKY 6 Pièces; STRAVINSKY 3 Easy Pieces
  (1 Pf./4 hands) ....MMO CD 3028 $29.98
____ BEETHOVEN Trios 8 in Eb & 11 in G ....MMO CD 3065 $34.98
____ BEETHOVEN Three Marches (1 piano/4 hands) ......MMO CD 3032 $29.98
____ BIZET Jeux d'enfants, op. 22(1 piano/4 hands) ..MMO CD 3043 $29.98
____ DEBUSSY Petite Suite (1P/4H)(1 piano/4 hands) ...MMO CD 3030 $29.98
____ DIABELLI Pleasures of Youth, op. 163 (1 piano/4 hands ..MMO CD 3046 $29.98
____ DVORAK 'Dumky' Trio A maj, op. 90 ....MMO CD 3037 $34.98
____ DVORAK Quintet A maj, op. 81 ....MMO CD 3038 $34.98
____ FAURE 'Dolly' Suite, op. 56 (1 piano/4 hands ...MMO CD 3029 $29.98
____ GRETCHANINOV On Green Meadow (1 piano/4 hands) ..MMO CD 3044 $29.98
____ HAYDN Trios, v. II: F/G/F#min(HobXV:6, 25, 26 ...MMO CD 3076 $39.98
____ MAYKAPAR First Steps, op. 29 (1 piano/4 hands) ..MMO CD 3041 $29.98
____ MENDELSSOHN Trio No. 1 in d, op. 49 ....MMO CD 3039 $34.98
____ MENDELSSOHN Trio No. 2 C min, op. 66 ....MMO CD 3040 $34.98
____ MOZART Complete Music (1 piano/4 hands) ....MMO CD 3036 $29.98
____ MOZART Piano Quartet No. 2 E-flat, KV493 ....MMO CD 6021 $29.98
____ MOZART Piano Quartet No.1 G min, KV478 ....MMO CD 6020 $29.98
____ MOZART Quintet E-flat, KV452....................MMO CD 3071 $39.98
____ POZZOLI Smiles of Childhood ....MMO CD 3045 $29.98
____ RACHMANINOV Six Scenes (1 piano/4 hands) ....MMO CD 3027 $29.98
____ RAVEL Trio A min ....MMO CD 3061 $34.98
____ SCHUBERT Fantaisie Fmin; Grand Son. Bb ....MMO CD 3047 $29.98
____ SCHUBERT Quintet A, op. 114, 'Trout' ....MMO CD 3087 $39.98
____ SCHUBERT Trio B-flat, op. 99 ....MMO CD 3066 $39.98
____ SCHUBERT Trio E-flat, op. 100 ....MMO CD 3067 $39.98
____ SCHUMANN Trio No. 1 D min, op. 63 ....MMO CD 3064 $39.98
____ SCHUMANN 'Bilder aus Osten'; Children's Ball ...MMO CD 3031 $29.98
____ TCHAIKOVSKY 50 Russian Folk Songs (1 piano/4 hands) MMO CD 3042 $29.98

Folk, Bluegrass and Country
____ You Write the Songs, vol. I:
  Country Styles Male/Female ....MMO CD 7021 $24.98

Inspirational Classics
____ Christmas Memories ....MMO CDG 1203 $24.98

Instrumental Classics with Orchestra
____ ARENSKY Conc. F maj, op. 2 ....MMO CD 3080 $39.98
____ C.P.E. BACH Conc. A min, Wq26 ....MMO CD 3059 $39.98
____ C.P.E. BACH Conc. D min, Wq23, H427 ....MMO CD 3091 $39.98
____ BACH B'burg 5 BWV1050 ....MMO CD 3054 $39.98
____ BACH Conc. 2 pianos C min;
  SCHUMANN Andante/Vars..............................MMO CD 3055 $39.98
____ BACH Conc. D min, BWV1052 ....MMO CD 3022 $39.98
____ BACH Conc. F min, BWV1056;
  J.C.Fr. BACH Conc. E-flat ....MMO CD 3021 $39.98
____ BACH 'Triple' Conc. A min; B'burg No. 5 (1st mvt)...MMO CD 3057 $39.98
____ BEETHOVEN Conc. No. 1, op. 15 ....MMO CD 6001 $39.98
____ BEETHOVEN Conc. No. 2, op. 19 ....MMO CD 6002 $39.98
____ BEETHOVEN Conc. No. 3 C min, op. 37 ....MMO CD 6003 $39.98
____ BEETHOVEN Conc. No. 4, op. 58 ....MMO CD 6004 $39.98
____ BEETHOVEN Conc. No. 5 E-flat, op. 73 ....MMO CD 6005 $39.98
____ BRAHMS Conc. No. 1 D min ....MMO CD 3009 $39.98
____ BRAHMS Conc. No. 2 B-flat, op. 83 ....MMO CD 6026 $39.98
____ CHOPIN Conc. E min, op. 11 ....MMO CD 3010 $44.98
____ CHOPIN Conc. F min, op. 21 ....MMO CD 3075 $39.98
____ GERSHWIN Rhapsody in Blue ....MMO CD 3083 $44.98
____ GLAZUNOV Conc. 1 Fmin, op. 92 ....MMO CD 3078 $39.98
____ Great Movie Concerti:
  Warsaw Concerto;Mozart; Rachmaninov ....MMO CD 3093 $39.98
____ GRIEG Piano Concerto ....MMO CD 6006 $39.98
____ HANDEL Conc. Grosso D; HAYDN Concertino C;
  J.C. BACH Conc. Bb ....MMO CD 3056 $39.98
____ HAYDN Conc. D maj, HobXVIII/11 ....MMO CD 3023 $39.98
____ Heart of the Concerto...........................MMO CD 3024 $29.98
____ KHACHATURIAN Piano Concerto ....MMO CD 6022 $49.98
____ LISZT Conc. No. 1; WEBER Konzertstuck ....MMO CD 3019 $39.98
____ LISZT Conc. No. 2; LISZT Hungarian Fantasia.....MMO CD 3020 $39.98
____ MACDOWELL Conc. No. 2 D min, op. 23 ....MMO CD 3090 $39.98
____ MENDELSSOHN Capriccio Brilliant;
  FRANCK Vars. Symphs................................MMO CD 3058 $39.98

____ MENDELSSOHN Conc. No. 1 G min, op. 25 ....MMO CD 3011 $39.98
____ MENDELSSOHN 'Double' Concerto
  for Piano, Violin & Strings ....MMO CD 6091 $39.98
____ MOZART Conc. No. 1 F KV37; No. 3 D KV40 ....MMO CD 6016 $39.98
____ MOZART Conc. No. 5 D K175/Rondo K382 ....MMO CD 3099 $39.98
____ MOZART Conc. No. 9 E-flat, KV271 ....MMO CD 3012 $39.98
____ MOZART Conc. No. 11 F, KV413 ....MMO CD 3097 $39.98
____ MOZART Conc. No. 12 A, KV414 ....MMO CD 3013 $39.98
____ MOZART Conc. No. 14 E-flat, KV449 ....MMO CD 3073 $39.98
____ MOZART Conc. No. 17 G, KV453 ....MMO CD 3085 $39.98
____ MOZART Conc. No. 18 B-flat, KV456 ....MMO CD 6017 $39.98
____ MOZART Conc. No. 19 F, KV459 ....MMO CD 3081 $39.98
____ MOZART Conc. No. 20 D min, KV466 ....MMO CD 3014 $39.98
____ MOZART Conc. No. 21 C, KV467 ....MMO CD 3072 $39.98
____ MOZART Conc. No. 22 E-flat, KV482 ....MMO CD 6023 $39.98
____ MOZART Conc. No. 23 in A, KV488 ....MMO CD 3098 $39.98
____ MOZART Conc. No. 24 C min, KV491 ....MMO CD 3016 $39.98
____ MOZART Conc. No. 25 C, KV503 ....MMO CD 3092 $39.98
____ MOZART Conc. No. 26 D, KV537 ....MMO CD 3017 $39.98
____ MOZART Conc. No. 27 B-flat, KV595 ....MMO CD 3082 $39.98
____ Opera Arias for Piano & Orch ....MMO CD 3048 $29.98
____ RACHMANINOV Conc. No. 2 ....MMO CD 3007 $39.98
____ RACHMANINOV Conc. 3, op.30 ....MMO CD 3074 $44.98
____ RACHMANINOV Rhapsody on a Theme of Paganini.....MMO CD 3084 $44.98
____ RIMSKY-KORSAKOV Conc. C#min; ARENSKY Fantasia ..MMO CD 3086 $39.98
____ RUBINSTEIN Conc. 4 Dmin, op. 70 ....MMO CD 3079 $39.98
____ SAINT-SAENS Conc. No. 2 G min, op. 22...........MMO CD 6036 $39.98
____ SAINT SAENS Piano Conc.
  No.4 in C minor. F.Moyer, piano ....MMO CD 6044 $39.98
____ SCHUMANN Conc. A min, op. 54 ....MMO CD 3008 $39.98
____ SCHUMANN, CLARA Conc.
  in A minor, Op.7 F. Moyer, piano...................MMO CD 6028 $44.98
____ TCHAIKOVSKY Conc. No. 1, op. 23.................MMO CD 3026 $39.98
____ Themes from Great Piano Concerti ....MMO CD 3025 $29.98

Jazz, Standards and Big Band
____ 2+2=5: A Study Odd Times ....MMO CD 2045 $24.98
____ Adventures in N.Y. & Chicago Jazz ....MMO CD 6014 $29.98
____ April in Paris: Songs for a Sunday Afternoon ...MMO CD 16015 $34.98
____ Bacharach Revisited ....MMO CD 6033 $29.98
____ Blues Fusion for Piano ....MMO CD 3049 $24.98
____ BOLLING Suite for Flute and Jazz Piano Trio....MMO CD 3050 $44.98
____ From Dixie to Swing.............................MMO CD 3053 $29.98
____ Funkdawgs: Jazz Fusion Unleashed ....MMO CD 2032 $24.98
____ Isle of Orleans (Tim Laughlin N.O.Jazz Band) ...MMO CD 6029 $29.98
____ Jazz Trios Minus You ....MMO CD 6009 $24.98
____ The Jim Odrich Experience ....MMO CD 3062 $24.98
____ New Orleans Classics (Tim Laughlin N.O.Jazz Band) ....MMO CD 6030 $29.98
____ Play Ballads with a Band ....MMO CD 8063 $29.98
____ Popular Piano Made Easy ....MMO CD 3063 $24.98
____ Sinatra Standards (Piano & Orch)................MMO CD 3069 $29.98
____ Jazz Jam ....MMO CD 3376 $29.98
____ STRETCHIN' OUT ....MMO CD 3060 $24.98
____ Studio Call: Film Scores ....MMO CD 2071 $24.98
____ Studio Call: Jazz/Fusion ....MMO CD 2081 $24.98
____ Studio Call: Pop/Country ....MMO CD 2096 $24.98
____ Studio Call: Rock/Funk ....MMO CD 2091 $24.98
____ Studio Call: Top 40 'MOR' ....MMO CD 2061 $24.98
____ Studio City ....MMO CD 2025 $24.98
____ Swing with a Band...............................MMO CD 8064 $29.98
____ Take One (minus Piano) ....MMO CD 2015 $24.98

Latin Classics
____ Brazilian Bossa Novas (Jim Odrich) ....MMO CD 16011 $34.98

Rock 'n' Roll
____ Weekend Warriors, vol. 1........................MMO CD 7131 $24.98
____ Weekend Warriors, Vol.2........................MMO CD 7132 $24.98

Student Series
____ Art of Popular Piano Playing, v. I (Vinson Hill)...MMO CD 3033 $24.98
____ Art of Popular Piano Playing, v. II (Vinson Hill) ...MMO CD 3034 $24.98
____ 'Pop' Piano For Starters (Student Level) ....MMO CD 3035 $24.98

MMO 6044

MUSIC MINUS ONE
50 Executive Boulevard • Elmsford, New York 10523-1325
914-592-1188 • e-mail: info@musicminusone.com
www.musicminusone.com

ISBN 978-0-9916347-4-3